BLIND? WHO? ME?

A true story

Illustrated by Tiffany Lee Huey

MARILYN ZIMMERMAN

NEWMAN SPRINGS PUBLISHING
320 Broad Street
Red Bank, NJ 07701

First originally published by Newman Springs Publishing 2023

ISBN 978-1-68498-703-0 (Paperback)
ISBN 978-1-68498-704-7 (Digital)

Printed in the United States of America

Hello!

My name was Tippy, and I want you to get to know me.
I was amazing!
(I *think!*)

At first, my mother could not take care of me and my sister. Our eyes hurt. We didn't like to have sore eyes.

2

One day, we were loaded in a box (my sister and me) and taken away.

That's when we met some nice people who saw we could not see. Our eyes were *so* sore—*bad* sore!

We were put to sleep for a nap, and we woke up without our eyes.

No eyes! Can you imagine? No eyes and it was hard to breathe out of our noses—but really, our eye places did feel better.

What could happen next?
We did not know.
A girl took sis and me to her house
and put us in a cage. It was warm. We
had lots of food and were being petted.
Oh, we liked that!

Soon, we were let out of our cage to explore. Sis said she did not feel good— her tummy hurt. I thought she would get better, but she was gone. She never cuddled next to me again.

I had ignored the other big cats, but now I went to find them. Most of them growled at me and slapped my face.

Oh! There was one big boy who kind of liked me.

I want to be just like *him*.

I made him mad at times because I teased him.

I would jump on him, so he would stay outside more.

I found out that his name was Koko. I loved him!

There was another cat. She was little. She acted like she was afraid of me—so I chased her and chased her some more. It was fun.

She got so mad at me. Her name was Beauty. Names were important because I could know who they (my people) were talking about.

I learned what she smelled like, so if she walked into my room, I knew it, and away I went after her. It was hard for her to hide.

I soon knew where everything was in the house like chairs, doors, tables, and *potty boxes*. Those were very important.

I also learned how high I had to jump for chairs (jumping was necessary).

I wanted to feel the ceiling. It was way up there.

So, first I got on the piano, went to the edge, reached until I felt the top of the cabinet, and let my paws feel up, up, up.

I had to stand on my tiptoes, and I felt the top of the cabinet.

My front legs were strong, so I reached and reached to get my claws on top and pulled.

Yes, I made it, and there was the ceiling!
The only problem was that I could not *get
down*! I cried, and my man friend came,
got on a chair, and lifted me down.

My people kept bringing baby kittens home. In fact, I gave them baths. I would hold them down with my paws so they could not get away.

I kept learning things. I loved people's food, and each Saturday, I would help with the pancakes—they were good. Hmm!

And another one of my ideas was to learn how far I had to jump from chair to chair without hitting the floor. I did it! Then, how far I could stand in the doorway, jump, and make it to the bed. Yes, that was hard, and I fell sometimes. But I learned, and sometimes other cats were there, and I landed on them.

Once I jumped from a banister at the back door. Oops!

That was not a good idea. I missed the step and hit my chin on the step—*OUCH!* That really hurt. I did not try that again.

My jumping still got me into more trouble.

There was a tree in the front yard, and the squirrels would tease me. You know,

Ha!

Ha!

Ha!

You can't get me!

So I decided to get him. Up the tree, he and I *went*.

Up the tree! It was really high—higher than the ceiling. All at once, the squirrel was gone, and I was high! How was I to get down? Then, I heard my man friend. He was telling me how to climb down backward. *But* that wasn't right. My legs went up—not down. So I listened to his voice. I knew where he was—

I had to get brave, and I knew he would catch me, I hoped. I jumped! My friend did not catch me because he knew I would grab him and hold tight and scratch him.

I landed feet first on the ground. (That is the way cats are supposed to land.)

Bump!

I guess I was all right. It did not even hurt much. You know what? I never climbed another tree!

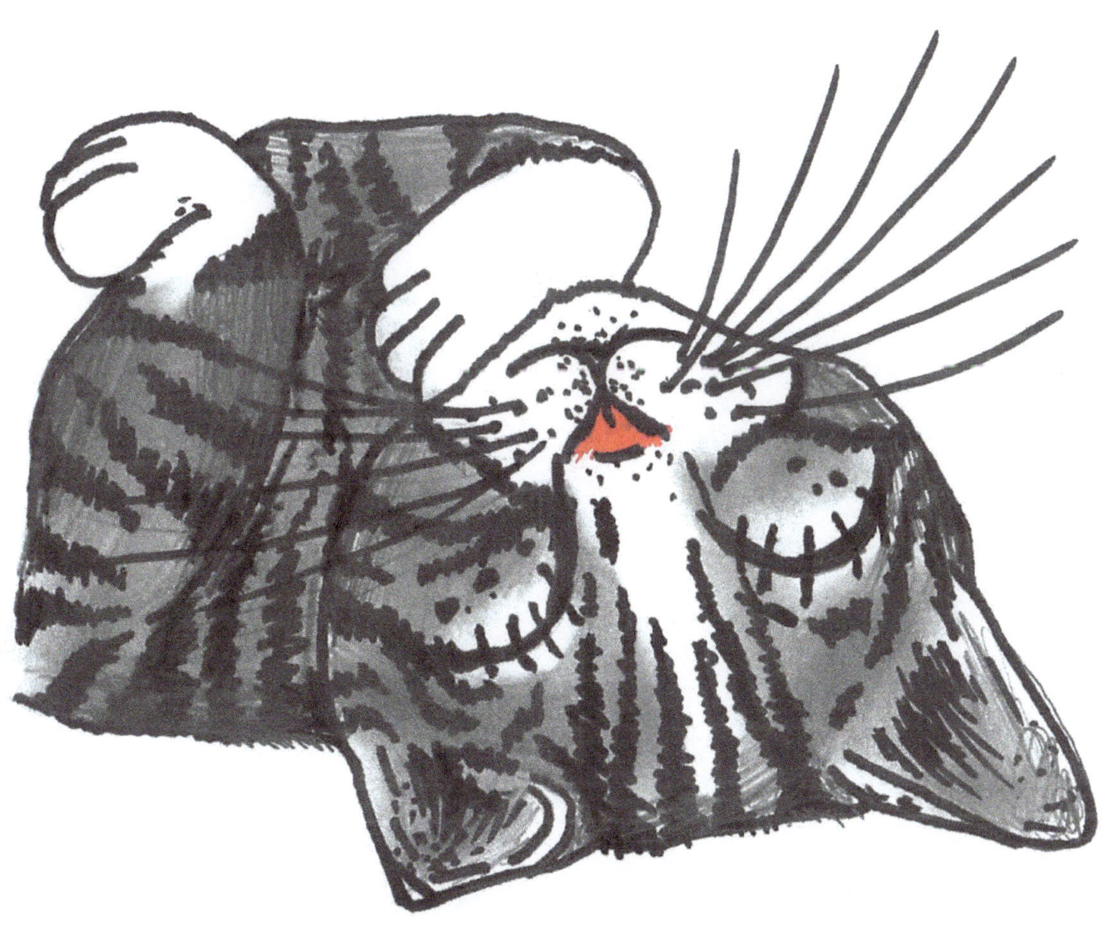

Birds, I wanted to catch one of those, too, but had to settle for catching flies in the windows: I could catch them and eat them, too.

Oh, I forgot. My people got me a buddy. He looked just like me (except he had eyes) and was my age. We had fun. We chased each other. He always got to be the leader. When I ran fast, I could not breathe right and stopped and had to pant.

Life was good.

But I still had not caught my squirrel.

Buddy caught a bird and gave it to me, so I learned about birds. I could hear them fly over my head. But I still wanted a squirrel. That ornery squirrel would run from me and stay almost within reach. I chased the squirrel into neighbors' yards. I still couldn't catch him.

Since I could not see, my ears got good; I could hear squirrels that would run in front of me to tease me, knowing I could not catch them. I would stay by the tree hoping they would not see me and come down. It never happened. I still chased the ones on the ground.

I guess I was not a good boy all the time. I tried, but that was hard.

My main problems were that I was proud of all the places I could go, and I wanted my friends to know. So can you guess what I did? You are right! I lifted my tail and *peed*. I got yelled at. I also got spanked, but I never learned.

And another place (I was really bad) that I caused trouble was the piano. Kids would come to play. I liked to hear it; in fact, I loved to play the keys, too. I even laid on the keys.

I wanted everyone to know I had been there—so yes, I did!

I *did*! I lifted my tail and peed on some music books. That was really *bad*.

Since I loved to go outside, a collar was put on me—but, no, not that. Now, the prissy cat (called "the queen") told me that cats wore collars; in fact, she did a long time ago and liked it. *Oh*, yes, she did. She did just *everything* right.

So I tried the collar. It didn't work.

I would get scolded, but I knew where I was—I think I only got lost once. But—I wanted a squirrel!

Then the squirrels started to go across the street. I knew I was not to go there. So I would sit by the street and wish.

My people would remind me to stay in the yard.

But maybe I could cross just *once*.
I did! *Wham!*
I was very special. My buddy misses me.
He saw where I was put on the ground.
All my friends knew what I had done.

I went over the kitty rainbow.

Rainbow Bridge
Just this side of heaven is a place called
the Rainbow Bridge. When an animal dies
that has been especially close to someone
here, that pet goes to the Rainbow Bridge
(copied).

My family misses me.
My people friends said I have new eyes
now, and I am with Jesus.

ABOUT THE AUTHOR

Marilyn Zimmerman has been a Methodist minister's wife, public school teacher (many grades and music), private piano instructor, museum guide, church choir director and wore many more hats in her spare time. Marilyn and her husband, Paul, raised 4 children in Indiana and Ohio during the 1960s through the 1980s. During the last 30 years, she has volunteered with local humane societies and fostered countless orphaned kittens. Books are very important to Mrs. Zimmerman, hence her newest "hat" – the author of a children's book.